Are you a Snail?

SRAonline.com

SRA

Printed in the U.S.A.

Send all inquiries to:
SRA/McGraw-Hill
4400 Easton Commons
Columbus, OH 43219-6188

ISBN 978-0-07-612268-4
MHID 0-07-612268-9

11 12 BRP 25

The McGraw-Hill Companies

Are you a Snail?

Judy Allen and Tudor Humphries

McGraw Hill SRA

Columbus, OH

Are you a snail?

If you are, your life began in an egg like one of these.

When you hatch, you look like this.

This is your mother.

You are much smaller
than your mother.

You are very, very small,
but you will grow.

You have two horns and two eyes on stalks.

You can pull your eyes right down inside the stalks and into your head if you need to.

You are slimy. You are VERY slimy.

You have a shell with a beautiful pattern on it.

You have no legs and only one foot, but it is a strong foot.

The slime on your strong foot helps you slide along.

Wherever you go, you leave a silvery, slimy trail.

You like damp places.

You like to be outside when it has rained.

You have a big, rough tongue right inside of your mouth. Use it to rip pieces off of leaves and eat them.

Watch out for thrushes.

Thrushes are dangerous.

They like to eat snails.

They know how to break the shells off,
and they don't mind the slime.

Hide in the daytime. Go out at night
when the thrushes are asleep.

Look out for foxes.

Foxes are dangerous.

Hungry foxes eat snails, and they don't mind the slime either.

Foxes go out at night, but you can't hide at night because you need to eat sometime. Just be careful.

Do not go where humans go.
You could get squashed. You move too slowly to get out of the way.

Humans don't like you because you eat their plants. They might put poison or sharp gravel in the garden.

It hurts to walk on gravel.
Also, it sticks to your slime.

And poison? Poison is poisonous!

You may meet someone who

looks like this.

It is not a snail whose shell has fallen off. This is a slug.

The winter cold makes you sleepy. Find a safe place.

Your slime hardens into a door in your shell.

The spring warmth wakes you. Dribble on the inside of your shell door. It melts away.

Slime off and find food.

However, if you look a little

or this

Like this

or this

or this

you are
not a snail.

You are . . .

. . . a human child.

You have no shell on your back.
You have no horns and your
eyes are not on stalks.

But you can do a lot of things that snails can't do.

You are not afraid of thrushes or foxes.

Most humans like you.

Best of all, you are not
in the least bit
slimy.

Did You Know . . .

. . . the trail of a snail is broken, but the trail of a slug is one long line of slime.

. . . there are more than 60,000 different kinds of snails.

. . . this is a garden  snail, but there are other kinds that live in deserts or swamps, in ponds or rivers, or in the sea.

. . . the Giant
African snail
can grow very large.
The biggest one ever found was almost
16 inches long and weighed two pounds!

. . . snails belong to a family of creatures

called gastropods, which
means "stomach-foot."
So you could say a snail is a
stomach on
a foot.